AF368095

ALISON WELCH

THE FREEMASONS

Unveiling the Mysteries of Freemasonry
(2024)

Copyright © 2023 by Alison Welch

All rights reserved. No part of this publication may be reproduced, stored or transmitted in any form or by any means, electronic, mechanical, photocopying, recording, scanning, or otherwise without written permission from the publisher. It is illegal to copy this book, post it to a website, or distribute it by any other means without permission.

First edition

This book was professionally typeset on Reedsy.
Find out more at reedsy.com

Contents

1

Introduction

Who truly governs the world? Some assert that there exists a clandestine group of men manipulating governments globally, orchestrating events from the shadows. These unseen puppeteers are intertwined with conspiracy theories worldwide, spanning from the assassination of John F. Kennedy to the tragic events of September 11, 2001, and beyond. Often, if you trace these conspiracies back to their roots, you will encounter a singular entity: the Freemasons.

But who are the Freemasons, really? Those subscribing to conspiracy theories might envision them as masterminds behind every significant geopolitical occurrence worldwide. However, to others, they are merely a social fraternity, an exclusive club engaged in community service. This book takes a distinctive approach.

Where did the Freemasons originate? In these pages, we explore the connections between the Freemasons and one of history's most renowned organizations, the Knights Templar. Could the Templars have laid the groundwork for the Freemasons? Did they establish this secretive society seeking retribution for their downfall? Did they inspire an English rebellion solely to vanquish their adversaries? Over the span of centuries, we delve into the evidence—should it exist—that unveils the links between these two enigmatic groups.

Due to their extreme secrecy, people often project their beliefs onto this covert society. However, within these pages, we strive to adhere strictly to the facts. Sometimes, these truths can be more astonishing than any speculation or theory. Delve into this narrative and uncover the concealed truths of the ancient Freemasons.

2

Chapter 1 :In the Beginning

The mysterious origins of the Freemasons have perplexed scholars and enthusiasts for centuries. Debates about when and by whom this secretive order was founded have given rise to numerous conflicting theories, debunked ideas, and even outright fabrications. The question of the Freemasons' origin is monumental. While contemporary Freemasonry might operate independently from the actions of a secretive society formed centuries ago, some argue that the ideologies, direction, and objectives of the Freemasons were set by the order's founding members. To truly comprehend the Freemasons, understanding their origins is essential.

However, this doesn't mean adhering to a single theory. On the contrary, the diverse origin narratives of the Freemasons can shed light on the fractured and controversial opinions about this enigmatic organization. The version of the origin story one chooses to believe often reflects personal biases and opinions. For instance, individuals who view the Freemasons as an extension of the Knights Templar might be more inclined to believe in the order guarding ancient secrets. Conversely, those who perceive the Freemasons as an 18th-century gentlemen's club are less likely to embrace the order's more contentious aspects. Exploring these varied origin stories enables us to grasp the wide spectrum of opinions about the Freemasons.

By delving into the history of the Freemasons, we gain unique insights into their contemporary existence. While not every historical account of the Freemasons is accurate, the fact that these stories have influenced public perception provides valuable insight. By discerning between true and false narratives, we can form our own opinions and develop a more comprehensive understanding. The truth often resides in the middle ground; the Freemasons' story is a murky, covert narrative painted in shades of gray. Without clear-cut heroes and villains, some find it challenging to grasp the reality of the situation. Therefore, we must explore every facet of Masonic history, delving into the nuances rather than merely focusing on the highlights.

3

Chapter2: Embarking on the Journey

Beginning our exploration from the very origins becomes essential, especially when the age of the Freemasons' Order is a subject of debate, making narrating their complete history a challenging task. In situations like these, adopting a chronological approach proves beneficial. Even though the early history of the Masons involves diverse groups, some entirely unaware of the term 'Freemasons,' delving into this background equips us with a richer understanding when the central figures enter the scene. Freemasonry didn't emerge as a fully developed entity; rather, its establishment (whenever that might have occurred) resulted from various influences and events. Global happenings converged, leading to the formation of the Freemasons. To truly grasp the order's origins, delving into this historical backdrop in depth becomes imperative. This entails traveling back several centuries to a world starkly different from our modern society.

The tale of Freemasonry is steeped in legends. For centuries, the Freemasons simply existed, their origins shrouded in mystery. Although people knew of their existence, little was known about their origins or the reasons behind their formation. However, this began to change in the late seventeenth century. Masons of that era began questioning their own beginnings, sparking an inquiry into their origins. Over time, this historical investigation expanded to include outsiders and skeptics of Masonry. Consequently, a more comprehensive, rigorous, and historical profile of the group started to emerge. Yet, the specifics remain fiercely debated. To trace the oldest verifiable origins, we must journey back to medieval times.

In any research venture online about the Masons lasting more than ten minutes, one name continually resurfaces—the Knights Templar. Curiously, they are intricately entwined in the Masons' narrative. However, this connection is often disputed. What is certain is that the Knights Templar are acknowledged for their role in the Freemasons' formation. Regardless of its veracity, given the widespread acceptance of this theory, delving into the Knights Templar's history becomes crucial. Understanding this group's story provides insight into the reasons people readily associate them with the Masons and their history. The Knights Templar's history is complex and contentious in its own right, yet undeniably fascinating.

Beginning the Journey

Starting from the very inception becomes crucial, especially when the age of the Freemasons' Order remains a topic of debate, making recounting the complete story challenging. In situations like these, adopting a chronological approach proves valuable. Even though the early history of the Masons involves entirely distinct groups, some unaware of the term 'Freemasons,' delving into this background provides a deeper understanding when the central figures come into play. Freemasonry did not emerge fully developed; instead, the formation of the order (whenever it happened) was the outcome of various influences and events. Global occurrences conspired, leading to the establishment of the Freemasons. To truly fathom the order's origins, delving into this historical context in-depth becomes imperative. This entails journeying back hundreds of years to a world vastly different from our contemporary society.

The tale of Freemasonry is steeped in legends. For many centuries, the Freemasons simply existed. Although people were aware of their presence, little was known about their origins or the reasons behind their creation. However, this began to change toward the end of the seventeenth century. Masons of that era began questioning their own beginnings, sparking an inquiry into their origins. Over time, this historical exploration expanded to include outsiders and skeptics of Masonry. Consequently, a more comprehensive, rigorous, and historical portrayal of the group started to emerge. Yet, the specifics remain hotly contested. To trace the oldest verifiable origins, we must journey back to medieval times.

Engaging in online research about the Masons for more than ten minutes inevitably leads to encountering one name repeatedly—the Knights Templar. Interestingly, they are intricately linked to the Masons' narrative. However, this connection is often disputed. What is certain is that the Knights Templar are recognized for their role in the formation of the Freemasons. Whether true or not, given the widespread acceptance of this theory, delving into the Knights Templar's history becomes vital. Understanding this group's story provides insight into why people readily associate them with the Masons and their history. The Knights Templar's history is intricate and disputed in its own right, yet undeniably captivating.

4

Chapter 3: The Knights Templar

The Knights Templar have been the subject of countless books, fascinating the masses in a way few other organizations do, except perhaps the Freemasons. Given the remarkable fame and intrigue surrounding both groups, it's natural that they would be interconnected. This intertwining of their histories takes us back in time. To uncover the Knights Templar's authentic origins, we need to journey back to the turn of the previous millennium.

The tale begins amidst the Crusades, a Holy War that erupted between the Catholic Church and early Islam. The conflict stemmed from disputes over the sacred territory of Jerusalem, a city revered by Christianity, Islam, and Judaism alike. In 1095, Jerusalem was under Muslim rule, and the power struggle for the city intensified.

The situation was intricate, involving political conflicts and disagreements. The initial intent of the western invasion of the Holy Lands was to assist the Byzantine Emperor against the Seljuk Turks. However, as the Papacy and key Western states became involved, the campaign broadened into a wider effort to reclaim Jerusalem and its surrounding regions from Muslim control, which had lasted since the 7th century. Various motives drove the Crusaders, ranging from military campaigns to political obligations and church alliances.

The Crusaders, hailing from Britain, France, Germany, Italy, and other states, embarked on a grueling journey, encountering violence along the way, including a brutal attack on a Jewish community in the Rhineland. Their path was marked by sieges and captures of key cities and castles, leading them to Jerusalem. The First Crusade, a full-scale military operation, brought them to the Holy City in 1099. Outside the city, the Crusaders faced harsh conditions, running low on supplies and manpower, and morale plummeted.

After failed attempts to breach the walls using biblical strategies, the Crusaders faced a decisive moment. Learning of a Muslim army en route from Egypt, they launched a final assault. On July 15th, a dual-pronged attack led to the defenders fleeing the walls, allowing the Crusaders to breach Jerusalem's defenses.

Following these events came a horrifying massacre. The Crusaders had undertaken a years-long journey, spanning thousands of miles, sacrificing numerous comrades along the way, all with the singular aim of reclaiming Jerusalem. The brutality of this bloodbath became legendary, especially concerning the events on Temple Mount. Defenders sought refuge in this sacred site, pivotal for the major Abrahamic religions, housing the al-Aqsa Mosque, the Dome of the Rock, and the Dome of the Chain. Legend had it that Solomon, a biblical figure, built his temple here, a structure destroyed and rebuilt multiple times. For Muslims, it stood as the third most sacred site globally, believed to be the place where Muhammad ascended to heaven. As the Crusaders attacked, Temple Mount seemed a natural sanctuary.

Relentlessly, the Crusaders pursued and slew anyone they found. A brief pause was called by their leader, allowing those sheltering in the Al-Aqsa mosque to be spared. However, this respite was short-lived. The Crusader commanders waited until the streets of Jerusalem were soaked in blood before entering the mosque, mercilessly killing the occupants. With the Crusaders now in control, they established the early foundations of the Kingdom of Jerusalem, a city coming to terms with unparalleled bloodshed. Thousands lay dead, countless more were wounded. In a distant land far from home, the Crusaders began the challenging task of governing the Holy Land.

This was the backdrop against which the Knights Templar emerged. Following the violent conquest of Jerusalem, Christianity had gained dominion over one of its most sacred sites. Pilgrimage to this location became vital, allowing people to express their devotion to Jesus Christ. Traveling from France to Jerusalem, primarily on foot for the less privileged, or by horse for the affluent, and occasionally by boat for the fortunate elite, was arduous and perilous. Moreover, the violence unleashed during the Crusade did little to endear Christians to the local communities in the Levant region. While Jerusalem fell under Christian control, the surrounding areas remained far from secure.

Ravaged by bandits, thieves, and those harboring resentment for the violence inflicted upon Muslim communities by the Crusaders, Christian pilgrims faced grave dangers during their journeys. In some instances, highwaymen killed entire groups of hundreds of travelers. As the years passed, this violence escalated. Eventually, a decision was made to address this issue, offering protection to pilgrims on their way. That decision-maker was Hugues de Payens, a French knight who, in 1119, sought permission from the rulers of Jerusalem to establish a new society. De Payens envisioned a religious monastic order—a disciplined group of knights sworn to safeguard pilgrims. By 1120, his request was granted, leading to the formation of the Knights Templar.

The name of the order derived from their headquarters, a wing of the royal palace atop Temple Mount, situated within the captured mosque where city defenders had sought refuge before meeting their demise. It seemed unusual to grant such prime real estate to a fledgling group, marking the first of many mysteries associated with the Knights Templar.

Initially, the organization fulfilled a critical need for the nascent Christian government in the Holy Land. Alongside other monastic orders, the Templars acted as a makeshift standing army. Despite their diverse backgrounds and nationalities, the rulers of Jerusalem were finally able to project an organized professional military force, leading to the rapid growth of the Templars, whose significance was quickly acknowledged.

However, with the surge in numbers came a rise in wealth and political influence. Initially consisting of nine knights with limited funds, the order relied on donations from powerful Christian rulers. Their organization's complete title was 'Poor Knights of Christ and the Temple of Solomon,' emphasizing their supposed poverty. To reinforce this image, they adopted the symbol of two knights riding a single horse, symbolizing their poverty. But this state of poverty didn't last.

The Knights Templar cultivated influential connections, propelling them to prominence among the monastic knights in the Holy Land. Esteemed members of the church praised their deeds, leading to an official endorsement from the Vatican. This elevated the Templars beyond a mere localized military order, granting them a revered status worldwide. People across Europe began contributing lands, money, businesses, and even family members to the Templars. Wealthy families sent young males to join the Templars, adding to their resources. Their prosperity surged further when a papal decree, Omne Datum Optimum, exempted them from local laws, taxes, and authorities, making them answerable only to the pope and God. In just two decades, these knights from Temple Mount transformed into one of the world's most influential and affluent groups.

Over the years, the Templars became crucial to the power dynamics in the Near East. While their military victories were vital locally, their wealth had a more significant impact in Europe. Papal endorsements overflowed the Templars' coffers. One major income source was aristocrats entrusting their assets to the Templars during their absence for the Crusades. In return, the Templars managed these properties, taking a share of the profits. This arrangement ensured the nobleman's assets were cared for and returned upon his departure from the Holy Land. With diverse revenue streams, the Templars established a pivotal institution of the medieval era: the Bank of the Knights Templar.

In the years that followed their expansion, most new Templar recruits were not placed in military roles but in administrative positions. The reason was straightforward: a significant number of people, particularly wealthy aristocrats, traveled through the Holy Lands and preferred not to carry their riches due to the threat of bandits. Instead, they entrusted their wealth to the Templars, who had branches in major cities. Deposits made in these branches were documented with detailed letters specifying the provided wealth. Upon reaching Jerusalem, the travelers could visit another Templar office and make withdrawals. This system, akin to the modern banking setup, marked the early stages of what is now considered the first international conglomerate.

In a remarkably short period, the Knights Templar transformed from a group of nine impoverished knights into one of the world's most influential entities. Their wealth took various forms. Donations and profits enabled them to acquire land in Europe and the Middle East. They established farms, vineyards, and businesses, augmenting their financial resources. They constructed castles, cathedrals, and fortifications across Europe, expanding far beyond their original territories. Templar forts even reached as far as Portugal. They engaged in trade, manufacturing, farming, banking, and operated their fleet of ships in the Mediterranean. At one point, they even owned the entire island of Cyprus.

As the Knights Templar gained immense power, other nations started to pay attention. Initially dedicated to protecting pilgrims, by the end of the 12th Century, they had become one of the world's most formidable organizations. They were not subject to local laws, even in countries like France, Britain, and Germany. Answering only to the pope, countries harboring grievances against the Vatican began to view the Templars with suspicion.

Many theories about the Freemasons' power often center around the international banking community, labeling major banks as part of an international cabal responsible for various global events. This notion draws parallels with medieval suspicions of the Knights Templar and their banking traditions. Some people use the often tenuous connection between the Freemasons and the global banking community as an accusatory measure, echoing historical suspicions of the Templars.

In the late 12th Century, the Knights Templar were often seen as arrogant. Their rapid ascent from humble beginnings to becoming a major international player within a century fueled this perception. The original military leaders of the organization had passed away, and the new Grand Master, de Ridfort, was not well-liked by heads of state and powerful nobles. They viewed him and his organization as arrogant and out of touch.

Additionally, the balance of power in the Holy Land was shifting. While the Crusaders had captured Jerusalem earlier, their control over the surrounding area was weakening. Saladin, a skilled commander, successfully recaptured many vital sites in the Levant. The Templars, once a crucial symbol of Christian military power, were tainted by association with these failures. As Saladin's army achieved victories, people began to resent the Templars for their inability to maintain control over the Holy Land. When Saladin re-conquered Jerusalem in 1187, it provided ammunition to criticize the Templars further. The fact that the remaining Christian-held territory along the coast was owned by the Templars led to accusations that they were protecting their own interests rather than those of Christianity.

In the following century, significant power dynamics shifted in the region. By 1296, the Holy Land was deemed entirely lost as Muslim rulers from Egypt successfully eradicated Christian influence. In response, the Templars relocated their operations from the Levant to their holdings in Cyprus. Across Europe, discussions about another Crusade surfaced, prompting the Templars to focus on their expanding business ventures.

However, their adversaries remained persistent. One of their most formidable foes was King Philip IV of France, who held various grudges against the order. Philip resented the Templars' influence and their immunity to local laws, and he was deeply indebted to them. Desiring to fund his ongoing wars rather than embark on a Crusade, he coveted the Templars' wealth.

Philip's circumstances improved after two crucial events: the death of the King of England, leading to a weaker opponent, and the appointment of Pope Clement V, who was more sympathetic to Philip's cause. Early speculations arose about a potential new Crusade, a common ambition expressed by new popes. When Pope Clement V assumed his position, the Templars hoped for a chance to reclaim their diminishing wealth and influence in the Holy Lands. Eager to explore this opportunity, the Templars sent their Grandmaster, Jacques de Molay, to France, where Pope Clement resided.

Jacques de Molay, the aging Grandmaster of the Templars, arrived in France with plans to regain Jerusalem. Initially welcomed, he soon found himself deceived. Behind the scenes, Philip and Clement conspired to bring down the Templars. On October 13, 1307, authorities launched a sudden assault, arresting every Templar member in France. This date, Friday the 13th, became infamous as the original reason for considering it an unlucky day.

The Persecution and Exodus of the Knights Templar: A Journey from Suppression to Secrecy in Scotland's Shadows:

The arrests carried out against the Templars held profound significance, as those captured endured brutal torture and punishment. Within French prisons, authorities extracted confessions from the Templars, revealing their descent into an unholy institution tainted by the worship of false deities, un-Christian rituals, and immense sin. These confessions, obtained under dubious circumstances, were presented as evidence of the Templars' guilt, serving as grounds to dismantle the global organization of the Knights Templar.

France witnessed a swift and merciless campaign against the Templars, but this persecution was not universal. Despite the Pope's papal decree outlawing the order, some regions hesitated to take action. For instance, in England, King Edward II initially refrained from arresting all Templars and instead pleaded their innocence with the Vatican. Upon the Pope's reaffirmation of the order's condemnation, Edward reluctantly issued arrest orders in January 1308. However, during the three-month gap between these actions, many local Templars managed to evade capture, disappearing along with their riches, including jewels, precious metals, and detailed records.

Overnight, the Knights Templar became an illegal entity. As the French King seized Templar estates and assets for himself, the order's international network was forcibly dismantled. With members branded as devil-worshipping heathens, openly identifying with the organization became unprofitable. Those Templars who escaped torture and death were compelled to go into hiding, transforming the group into a clandestine society. In this dire situation, one of the few havens available to them was Scotland.

Scotland, like several other European nations, found itself in a precarious political position. Strained relations with England led to their isolation from the broader international community, distancing them from both Europe and the Pope's authority. While the rest of Europe relentlessly pursued the Templars, Scotland did not issue any arrest orders. Seizing this opportunity, many Templars, intent on concealing themselves during these tumultuous times, are believed to have fled north to Scotland, carrying whatever remnants of their extraordinary wealth they could salvage.

This is the point where theories about the Knights Templar start to diverge significantly for many people. At this juncture, a clear separation emerges between the documented history of the organization and the speculative possibilities that venture far from conventional narratives. While we can't delve deeply into the stranger aspects of the Templars here due to space constraints, the wide range of these possibilities forms the basis for understanding the Freemasons.

Much attention has been devoted to the Templars' wealth during this period. While some individuals view this wealth purely in financial terms, others propose that the Templars were concealing something far more intriguing. They raise questions: How did this small group of impoverished knights swiftly rise to power? How did they attain such legal immunity from the church? Some theories suggest that the answers lie back in Temple Mount. It's been hypothesized that the Templars' initial headquarters in Jerusalem held secrets beyond mere administration. Upon being granted offices in the holy buildings, the Templars began excavation. During this process, they allegedly discovered something profound. The exact nature of this discovery is as disputed as whether it occurred at all. The find has been theorized to be anything from a statue of Baphomet imbued with dark magical powers to the Ark of the Covenant, housing the original tablets bearing the Ten Commandments, or even the Holy Grail. Even the Grail's nature is debated, ranging from a simple cup used at the Last Supper to extensive documentation detailing the mortal lineage of Jesus Christ, including his earthly family and descendants up to modern times. Each of these items has been proposed as the key to the Templars' power, potentially explaining how they rapidly attained such a significant position.

Many historians have dedicated their lives to unraveling not only the fate of the Knights Templar but also the enigmatic secrets they safeguarded. However, to comprehend their connection to the Freemasons, it's necessary to consider what we've discovered about the Knights Templar and shift our focus a few years forward to the condition of England in the 14th century.

5

Chapter 4: The Uprising of the Commoners

Following Edward II's reign came Edward III, a period marred by continuous conflicts between high-ranking barons and other nobles, notably his association with a man named Piers Gaveston. This relationship sparked widespread outrage, leading to legislative chaos and a power struggle. Gaveston was eventually captured and executed by the barons, sparking prolonged conflict. Edward II attempted to quell issues in his kingdom and resolve disputes with Scotland, but complications arose as Gaveston had also angered France, creating problems on two crucial fronts. The conflict culminated in the English King's defeat by Scottish leader Robert the Bruce in 1314, causing enduring repercussions such as famine and strife in England. Criticism of Edward II intensified.

Despite efforts to appease his critics, Edward II faced extended disputes, betrayals, and executions in dealings with Scotland. He was compelled to sign a peace treaty with Robert the Bruce after his defeat. Similar challenges arose in his interactions with France. In 1325, Edward sent his wife, Isabella, to negotiate peace. Although she was a daughter of the French King and Edward's marriage was meant to foster peace, Isabella defied expectations. Instead of negotiating, she allied with a faction and invaded her own homeland. In 1326, with an army, Isabella waged war against Edward II. Fearing for his life and trapped between hostile forces, Edward fled to Wales. He was captured a few months later, compelled to relinquish his crown in January 1327, passing it to his fourteen-year-old son, Edward III. Less than a year later, the former king died under suspicious circumstances, likely assassinated at the behest of the new rulers.

Edward III's reign, spanning from 1327 to 1377, marked a period of significant success for England. Despite his youth when he ascended the throne, he ruled for fifty years, striving to establish England as a prominent player in European politics. While his predecessor had diminished England's influence, Edward III bolstered the country's military strength, engaging in prolonged battles against France, initiating the Hundred Years War, and achieving notable victories. However, domestic challenges arose, including the devastating impact of the Black Death, which claimed numerous lives and devastated towns and villages. In his later years, Edward III's health deteriorated, hindering his ability to govern. He passed away in 1377, and the crown was inherited by his ten-year-old grandson, Richard II, whose own father had died the previous year.

The question arises: why delve into this historical context in a book about the Freemasons? The upheaval in 14th-century England distracts attention from the mysterious disappearance of the Knights Templar. By Richard II's reign, the Templars had seemingly faded from memory. With a young king on the throne, England had become a major political power, seemingly overcoming threats from France and Scotland. It appeared that England was poised for a period of lasting success, but fate had other plans.

In the pre-Reformation era, the Catholic Church stood as one of the world's few international organizations, holding sway in nearly every European community. England was no exception, and the Church, tainted by corruption and greed, was a target of peasant unrest. This inherent conflict, between being a force for good and succumbing to corruption, mirrored a similar contradiction experienced by the exiled Knights Templar. Originally a Catholic militant organization, an extension of the church's military might, the

Templars faced condemnation and conviction by the very institution they had vowed to protect. Some scholars argue that it was this Vatican decree that severed the ties between the church and the Templars. Following their exile, the Templars found themselves without a master, free to align with any faction they chose.

However, internal divisions within the Church itself deepened during this period. In 1377, Pope Gregory XI moved the papal residence from Avignon back to Rome, causing dissatisfaction among his cardinals. The Church, having adopted a French character during its stay in France and aligning closely with the French monarchy, faced disapproval from the French faction. After Gregory's death, the appointment of an Italian pope led to riots in Rome. This event triggered the Great Schism of 1378, the most significant split in the Church's history. The Church divided into two factions: one led by Pope Urban VI in Rome and the other by Pope Clement VII in Avignon, supported by different cardinals and countries. France, Scotland, Portugal, Spain, and several German territories sided with Clement VII, while England, Poland, Hungary, most of the Holy Roman Empire, and those opposed to France supported Urban VI. Each faction excommunicated the priests of the other, declaring itself the true Church.

Amidst this spiritual conflict, France and England found themselves engaged in both a conventional war and a theological battle. Urgently needing funds, England imposed the poll tax in 1377, causing outrage. The peasantry, whose position had shifted due to the Black Death, had become more in-demand, leading to improved wages. However, landowners, now more powerful due to a reduced workforce, conspired to pass laws limiting peasant payments and pushing wages back to pre-plague levels. Additionally, efforts were made to bind people permanently to specific lords, solidifying serfdom in law. These measures led to escalating tensions between the classes.

In the late spring of 1381, long-standing grievances reached a boiling point, sparking a rebellion in Kent and Essex famously known as the Peasants'

Revolt. Led by figures like Wat Tyler, the peasants assembled in large numbers, demonstrating their discontent. They demanded the end of serfdom, the oppressive feudal system that made them subservient to the landowners' whims. Their anger escalated to the extent that they burned down Savoy Palace and killed members of the King's court. Faced with this massive uprising, the young King and his advisors sought refuge in the Tower of London, realizing they lacked the strength to confront the thousands of peasants directly. Negotiation became their only option.

The King, only fourteen years old and reliant on his inner circle's counsel, found his position precarious. Financial stability eluded his kingdom due to the costly wars waged by his grandfather, draining the treasury. Corruption had also seeped into the court, exacerbating the crisis. In response, the crown imposed new and oppressive taxes, including the poll tax, which served as a catalyst for the rebellion. Both the barons and landowners, as well as the cash-strapped King, shared the blame. England, desperate for funds and besieged by challenges, erupted in revolt. Complicating the situation, there appeared to be some level of planning behind the uprising.

Many historians have suggested that the Peasants' Revolt was not a spontaneous outburst. Whispers of rebellion and discontent had been nurtured throughout the country, and various sources of dissatisfaction coalesced. Influential figures like John Ball, a leader among priests sympathetic to the poor, played a crucial role in fanning the flames of revolt. As these sentiments spread, communities across the country were urged to rise up, resulting in an assembly of as many as 100,000 peasants expressing their dissatisfaction with the crown.

The initial signs of the uprising became apparent when tax collectors were assaulted during their duties. In one incident, a local lord tried to forcefully collect taxes and have around a hundred defiant peasants arrested. However, the officers were attacked, and the lord narrowly escaped to London. In response, the government sent a larger force to quell the unrest, but the enraged masses counterattacked with renewed determination. Prosecutors were not only captured but also beheaded. This unrest began in Essex and soon spread to Kent and the areas around London. The mob grew in size, drawing people from villages and towns across the country, marching against the king.

Amidst this large assembly, one man, Walter (or Wat) Tyler, emerged as a leader. Without much apparent reason, many swiftly turned to him for guidance, and the revolt became known as Wat Tyler's Revolt. However, little is known about Tyler, his origins, or his specific grievances. Why did thousands of men suddenly accept him as their leader? It's challenging to discern, although some suggest a deeper level of understanding among the rebels than what might be evident today.

As Wat Tyler and his followers moved through Canterbury, beheading "traitors" along the way, similar disturbances occurred in Essex. On the day Tyler and his men attended a mass in Canterbury Cathedral, the men from Essex were burning down a significant building owned by the Knights Hospitallers. This building had historical significance, having belonged to the Knights Templar until they were outlawed and expelled. Afterward, it fell into the hands of the Hospitallers, who profited considerably from the Templars' downfall, inheriting their properties and wealth. Over the following days, rebel forces targeted many important Hospitallers' structures, suggesting a broader societal upheaval. Could it be a coincidence that the rebels were eager to attack the sworn enemies of the Knights Templar? Here, the threads of history began to intertwine, revealing connections dating back to the Crusades centuries earlier.

On June 11th, both groups of rebels made a significant decision to march towards the capital with their combined force exceeding 100,000 individuals. Despite their scattered origins and lack of formal training, historians were astounded by the determination and discipline exhibited by these rioters. Their journey covered a daunting seventy miles, accomplished in just two days, with both groups arriving in London around the same time. The level of coordination led many to speculate that this movement was premeditated rather than a random occurrence.

At this critical juncture, the teenage king sought refuge within the Tower of London, accompanied by his most trusted advisors, including the Archbishop of Canterbury, the king's treasurer (a Hospitaller member), and a man named Henry Bolingbroke, the future King of England. Earls, barons, and various aristocrats, all fearing the wrath of the uprising, were also present within the Tower.

By June 12th, the rebels gathered in what is now East London, marching across the river and moving through Southwark. As more people joined their ranks from different parts of the city, these rebellious groups took it upon themselves to ransack and burn palaces, with a particular focus on destroying aristocratic records of lineage and genealogy used to enforce serfdom. Prisons were stormed, and all inmates were set free. Inside the Tower of London, the young king witnessed his city in flames. In response, he dispatched messengers to the rebels, inquiring about their demands. The reply he received indicated that the rebels aimed to save the king from the treacherous advisors who surrounded him and were allegedly destroying the country. The king pleaded for a meeting, urging the rebels to cease their destruction so he could listen to their grievances in full.

The rebels agreed, positioning themselves on both sides of the river - those from Kent on the south side and those from Essex on the north. The king departed from the Tower of London aboard his royal barge, slowly drifting down the river to meet the rebels. Halfway through his journey, his advisors convinced him to halt. Once it became apparent that the king had stopped, the rebels sent out their demands directly to the barge. Their demands included a list of men to be executed, many of whom were aboard the royal barge at that very moment, such as the prior of the Hospitallers and the Archbishop of Canterbury. Predictably, the king's council advised against such action. From the shore, the rebels witnessed the king's barge turning back towards the Tower.

The rebels made their way into the heart of the city, and curiously, neither of the gates they approached happened to be guarded. Unopposed, they strolled straight through. Rather than pillaging and laying waste to everything in their path, they proceeded directly to Fleet Street, a significant part of London that happened to house a prison. There, they launched an attack, liberating all the inmates.

Close by were two forges formerly owned by the Knights Templar but now managed by the Hospitallers. The rebels, as before, vented their anger on these forges, completely destroying both. While marching through the city toward the Savoy Palace, the mob only halted to assault any building they could verify as belonging to the Hospitallers. Many structures were damaged, but none suffered the mob's wrath as severely as the Savoy Palace. Priceless artworks, furniture, tapestries, and numerous other valuable items were irreparably ruined. After their rampage, the rebels set the palace ablaze, ensuring the destruction by moving gunpowder kegs inside.

With Savoy Palace reduced to ruins, the rebels once again turned their focus to structures that might be owned or operated by the Knights Hospitaller. Any such property located between the Thames and Fleet Street was vandalized and set on fire. Records were set alight, and any lawyers who attempted to intervene were killed. One Hospitaller property that escaped much of the devastation was a small church. Nevertheless, the rebels entered and gathered any records they could find, burning them in the street. Perhaps not coincidentally, this church had previously belonged to the Knights Templar, and it was one of the few targeted buildings that remained partially intact. Compared to the Hospitaller headquarters in Clerkenwell, which was rendered beyond repair, the survival of the Templars' former church seemed somewhat miraculous.

The rebels pressed on with their campaign, traversing the city, freeing prisoners, burning records, and singling out Hospitaller properties. One group, after being denied an audience with the king when they petitioned the Tower of London, laid siege to the fortress, seemingly unconcerned that it was among the most defensible structures in England.

Citywide proclamations condemned anyone affiliated with the Exchequer or the Chancery, two tax-collecting authorities in the country, to death. To find evidence of this alleged crime, the presence of ink on a man's fingers was deemed sufficient proof of guilt. Given that most literate men had received their education from the church, it was no coincidence that a significant portion of the casualties were members of the clergy.

The king appeared deeply shocked and utterly unprepared to respond to the uprising. Without an army to confront the massive rebel gathering, lacking the funds to appease the crowds, and unable to organize quickly enough to counter such a well-coordinated rebellion, the king found himself in a quandary. Instead of relying on a show of strength, he had to resort to deception. On June 14th, it was publicly announced that the king was willing to meet with the rebel leaders and fully concede to all their demands. This message was broadcast by town criers throughout the city for everyone to hear.

As a meeting location, the king and his advisors chose Mile End, an area with open fields just outside the city walls. The primary objective was to lure the rebels out of the city. To a large extent, this plan worked, as a significant portion of the rebel forces followed the king beyond the city walls. However, not everyone left. Wat Tyler and a few hundred men remained in the city, armed and with their own agenda.

Even on the morning of the planned meeting, all was not well within the king's camp. Before they departed to meet the rebels, the Archbishop of Canterbury was caught attempting to escape down the Thames in a boat. Bystanders recognized him, and the resulting outcry from the riverbanks compelled the boatmen to retreat back to the Tower, foiling the archbishop's escape attempt.

The king proceeded to the meeting, accompanied by his trusted advisors. The historical records specify the people who were with him but remain silent on those members of the court who chose not to attend. In particular, there is no mention of Sir Simon Sudbury and Sir Robert Hales, that is, the Archbishop of Canterbury and the prior of the Knights Hospitaller. Whether they stayed in the Tower by choice or were ordered to do so remains unclear. There is also no information about who assumed leadership in the rebel camp that day, while prominent figures like Wat Tyler and John Ball stayed in the city, pursuing their secretive agenda.

Initially, the meeting at Mile End appeared promising. The rebels had two demands: first, the right to identify and execute anyone they considered a traitor to the king and the people; second, the abolition of serfdom, granting freedom to every Englishman. The king's response seemed reasonable. To the first demand, he agreed that 'traitors' should be executed, but only if they were proven guilty in a court of law. For the second request, he turned to a group of thirty clerks who had accompanied him, specifically appointed to draft legislation promptly.

While the meeting between the rebels and the king seemed to be proceeding smoothly, events unfolded in the city without regard for the negotiations. The rebel leaders, led by Wat Tyler, launched their attack. They had planned to seize and hold the Tower of London itself—a highly ambitious goal even under the best circumstances, let alone with only a few hundred poorly armed rebels. The Tower, already the most fortified building in the country, was guarded by hundreds of professional soldiers. It boasted a drawbridge, a portcullis, a heavy gate, and a vast array of weapons. Additionally, the troops inside the Tower were under the command of Robert Hales, the prior of the Knights Hospitaller, an experienced battle commander.

Nevertheless, Wat Tyler and his men launched their assault. Curiously, it appeared that the rebels had assistance from someone inside the Tower. Upon their arrival, they found the drawbridge lowered, the portcullis raised, and the gate wide open. Without facing any resistance, the rebels boldly entered the Tower of London, and surprisingly, no confrontations were documented.

Once inside, the rebels moved swiftly to capture their targets. Their first victim was the Archbishop of Canterbury, whom they discovered in the chapel. Dragging him outside, they mercilessly beat him before throwing him to the ground. Simultaneously, another group arrived with the defenseless Hospitaller. Holding both men captive, the rebels scoured the tower for others on their list: tax collectors, lords, and similar figures. After apprehending everyone they sought, the rebels escorted these men to Tower Hill. Before a frenzied crowd, they beheaded each one, mounting their severed heads on poles atop London Bridge. As a grim gesture of the former Archbishop of Canterbury's status, they affixed his distinctive mitre to his head.

Following these executions, the rebels fanned out across the city, hunting down others on their list—around 160 individuals in total—who they considered corrupt, treacherous, or who had opposed them. They also targeted those who spoke against them or praised the deceased.

Wat Tyler organized a special mission, selecting a small group of rebels and dispatching them toward Highbury with a specific objective: the destruction of a particular building owned by the Hospitallers. This structure, recently renovated by the order, was renowned for its opulence. News of this attack quickly reached the king and his advisors at Mile End. The planned meeting was abruptly abandoned, and the king hurried back to his residence in Castle Baynard, clearly avoiding a return to the Tower of London.

Meanwhile, the clerks tasked with drafting legislation continued their work, seemingly unfazed by the surrounding chaos. Before the king departed, many rebels seized pages from the clerks, carrying these royal decrees back to their hometowns.

The subsequent events are murky, poorly recorded in history. It appears that the king agreed to meet the rebels once more, this time at Smithfield, scheduled for the following day, June 15th. Before the meeting, the king attended mass at Westminster Abbey, with some rebels curiously observing the proceedings. During the service, they spotted a despised tax collector hiding in one of the chapels. Ignoring his pleas for mercy, they dragged him into the open and executed him in front of the crowd. The king then concluded the mass and proceeded to Smithfield.

At Smithfield, a significant number of rebels had gathered, standing on one side of the field, while the young king and his men lined up on the other. The exact events that unfolded are fiercely debated in historical accounts. Some sources claim that Wat Tyler, one of the leaders of the rebels, insulted the king, causing tension. In all likelihood, this incident provided the king and his men the pretext they needed to execute their predetermined plan.

The king signaled for the leader of the rebels, Wat Tyler, to approach him. To convey this request, the Mayor of London, William Walworth, was sent across the field. Suspicious of the situation and realizing he would be outnumbered and vulnerable far from his men, Tyler devised a hand signal. If implemented, it meant the rebels should immediately attack. Tyler, accompanied by only one man bearing his banner, ventured across the field.

It's worth noting that the accounts of what transpired next are primarily from government sources, as many eyewitnesses were likely not present. According to these official versions, Wat Tyler met with the king and reiterated his list of demands. This time, the demands had expanded; Tyler now sought the seizure of church property with the wealth distributed among the poor, numerous legal changes, and the appointment of a single bishop for all of England.

As Tyler enumerated his demands in front of the king, William Walworth discreetly drew his dagger. Approaching Tyler from behind, the mayor slashed his neck. A squire of the king joined the attack, stabbing Tyler twice. In an attempt to turn back toward his men, Tyler fell from his horse. The wounds proved fatal, and he succumbed to his injuries.

From the perspective of the rebels across the field, the situation was unclear. They had not witnessed the prearranged hand signal. Instead, they saw a rider approach from the distance. It was the king himself, the fourteen-year-old boy. He addressed the rebels, indicating his willingness to meet their demands and invited them to accompany him to Clerkenwell, where the Hospitaller palace still burned, to finalize their agreement. With that, the king rode away, leading his men and army.

The rebel forces were left bewildered after the death of Wat Tyler. Uncertain of their next move, some rebels ventured across the field to retrieve Tyler's dying body, taking him to a nearby hospital for treatment. After an hour of deliberation, the disorganized rebels eventually decided to heed the king's instruction and set out for Clerkenwell.

Unbeknownst to them, anti-rebellion groups were gathering strength, possibly motivated by the news of Wat Tyler's demise. Hundreds of individuals were mobilizing against the rebels. The Mayor, the king, and other authority figures rallied any able-bodied men to take up arms against the uprising.

Upon reaching Clerkenwell, the rebels immediately demanded that the king hand over those responsible for Wat Tyler's murder. As they presented their case to the king, an anti-rebellion mob gathered around them. Unnoticed by the rebels, these men gradually encircled them. The leader of the anti-rebellion group informed the king that they now had the upper hand, revealing the rebels' surrounded and outnumbered position. The king demanded the rebels disperse, warning them of consequences if they resisted.

Realizing the tables had turned, the rebel crowd began to scatter, lacking the previous organization. They dispersed in small groups, with John Ball, the preacher, leading one organized band back across London Bridge, retreating from the city they had triumphantly entered just days before.

Mayor William Walworth located Wat Tyler in a hospital near Smithfield, where he was being treated for his wounds. Despite Tyler's likely mortal injuries, Walworth took no chances. He pulled Tyler from the hospital bed onto the street, where, like many other rebel victims, Tyler was beheaded. His head replaced those of the king's men on the poles above London Bridge.

Several members of the king's inner circle received knighthoods for their role in repelling the mob from the city. However, the problem was not entirely resolved. Outside London, widespread discontent persisted. Anger at taxes and mistreatment of the poor was not limited to Essex and Kent; incidents occurred across the country before and after the Peasants' Revolt.

Reports from Suffolk revealed a local preacher rallying disgruntled locals to burn down a corrupt nobleman's residence, expel clergymen from a monastery that held people in serfdom, and destroy records while plundering wealth. Notable figures, such as the chancellor of Cambridge University, faced execution for corruption. Rebels seized Nottingham Castle and other castles, ransacked aristocratic homes, and executed people in multiple regions, targeting properties belonging to the Hospitallers.

There was evident communication and organization among the rebels. Uprisings took place in Yorkshire and other regions nearly simultaneously. The aftermath of the rebellion was significant; authorities cracked down on any signs of disorder and discontent across the country. The rebels' promises were broken, arrests were made, and inquisitions conducted not only to identify the rebels but also to uncover any covert connections behind the revolt. Suspicion lingered that someone was orchestrating the uprising.

Although this discussion began with historical events seemingly unrelated to modern Freemasonry, understanding these ancient incidents sheds light on the secretive operations of clandestine organizations. Exploring the Knights Templar and the Peasants' Revolt provides insight into the controversy surrounding modern Masonry. In the next chapter, the interconnectedness between these historical events and contemporary Freemasonry will be explored in greater depth.

6

Chapter 5: The Hidden Network

The aftermath of the Peasants' Revolt was marked by brutality. While historical accounts often carried biases tailored to please the king, delving deeper allows us to uncover potential truths obscured by propaganda. For instance, investigations led by aldermen and state officials hinted at the existence of a mysterious organization. Amidst the genuine outrage felt by many rebels towards the authorities, some referred to a clandestine group called the Great Society. This enigmatic entity was mentioned in records, dispatching representatives and messengers, fueling discord, and playing a role in inspiring the rebellion.

In the context of a discussion about the Freemasons, acknowledging the Great Society's existence becomes crucial. The connections we've explored so far in this historical narrative will soon become evident. The objective is to establish a link between the earliest Knights Templar, the Great Society orchestrating the Peasants' Revolt, the integration of Freemasons into broader society, and their eventual acceptance as an integral part of modern civilization. It's essential to understand these connections without falling into the trap of conspiracy theories suggesting a single organization has dominated Western society's political landscape for centuries. Instead, a critical examination of secret societies, with the Freemasons being the most renowned in the contemporary world, is necessary.

To pursue this quest for knowledge, we must inquire: who were the members of the Great Society? When revisiting the official account of the Peasants' Revolt, certain discrepancies emerge. The role attributed to the young king, Richard II, stands out. Official narratives depict him as a decisive leader who inspired men and crushed the rebellion. However, reality paints a different picture. Richard did not truly rule until the age of twenty-three. Before that, an elected council of regents governed the kingdom on his behalf. Unofficial descriptions of Richard portray him as a timid, stuttering teenager, far from the confident leader capable of addressing a rebel army after defeating their leader.

The Tower of London's role raises suspicion due to several perplexing factors. It was, arguably, the most defensible location in England, especially against a small group of rebels like Wat Tyler's. The ease with which Tyler and his men entered, combined with his lack of interest in using it as a headquarters after his executions, raises questions. If the rebels' meeting with the king held promise, why attack the Tower at all? It appears that the real purpose of the meeting at Mile End was to remove the king from the city, leaving the Tower vulnerable to Tyler's attack. This raises the possibility that the Tower itself was the true target.

Another puzzling aspect is the decision to leave key members of the king's council in the Tower, only for the rebels to execute them. While the Archbishop of Canterbury's situation is somewhat understandable, Robert Hales, the skilled battle commander and leader of the Knights Hospitallers, should have accompanied the king to face such a significant threat. Hales' military expertise and reputation as a formidable soldier make it baffling that he was left behind.

Numerous questions arise: Why didn't the king return to the Tower after the meeting? Was it mere chance that his household servants were conveniently in place? These circumstances suggest that the decisions might have been orchestrated by the king's council of regents, rather than the king himself. It implies that they likely prearranged these events, guiding Richard's actions throughout.

Examining the aftermath of the rebellion sheds light on the king's actions. Many rebels received royal pardons, and towns that had harbored them were granted amnesty, allowing them to resume their normal activities. However, this leniency did not apply universally. A specific list of 287 men was excluded from the amnesty, and these individuals, including figures like Henry de Newark and Richard de Melton, seemed to vanish completely. Despite being named on the list and mentioned in a royal decree, these men, along with others, disappeared without a trace. In a time when travel between towns was challenging, the sudden disappearance of individuals beyond local borders raised significant concerns. The pattern of disappearance among the 287 men led some historians to draw parallels with the Knights Templar's vanishing act seventy years earlier. Both groups faced condemnation, were pursued by authorities and the church, and urgently needed shelter and sustenance. The apparent ease with which these men found refuge suggests a pre-planned escape strategy, possibly involving safe houses and hideouts provided by an organization known as the Great Society.

Additionally, the church's response to the rebellion is noteworthy. Despite the rebels' brutal act of beheading the Archbishop of Canterbury, his successor did not seek direct retaliation. Instead, the church initiated a campaign against heresy, echoing the crime for which the Templars were accused decades earlier. However, the true impact of the rebellion on the church would only become evident later. The doubts and resentments sown during the Revolt would eventually flourish during the Protestant Reformation, marking a significant turning point for the church.

As previously mentioned, the Peasants' Revolt harbors its most significant enigma: the existence of a covert organization orchestrating events behind the scenes. Historians generally agree that there was indeed a clandestine network at play during the rebellion, although the specifics and extent of this mysterious group remain subjects of debate. One central query is whether this organization emerged solely in response to the 1381 political climate or if it was a pre-existing entity acting on longstanding grudges and agendas that spanned centuries. In essence, was it a reactionary formation or an established entity? Could the 287 men excluded from the amnesty have been potential members of this covert group? Is it conceivable that this obscure organization was the lingering remnant of the Knights Templar, who had been in hiding for seventy years?

All signs point to a meticulously planned and large-scale organized response to the government. Recovered documents from sheriffs and bailiffs indicate the authorities' belief in secret meetings leading up to June. Such coordination demanded substantial effort—establishing a network of trustworthy individuals, vetting members, and determining agendas and meeting locations. This task is formidable even within a confined geographic area, let alone spanning medieval England.

The organization fueling the Peasants' Revolt must have been disciplined, astute, motivated, and well-prepared. Creating and maintaining a clandestine communication system across the country without detection suggests a level of sophistication beyond the reach of the average peasant. Even when collaborating across two or three towns, the resources available to ordinary working people were likely insufficient for such an undertaking. Considering the majority of peasants were illiterate, the challenges of organizing such a complex operation become even more evident.

It's essential to note that any secretive organization operating in such a manner would inevitably face opposition from spies, traitors, and double agents. To counter this, covert signals were employed—these could be gestures, prearranged conversation cues, or specific mannerisms. The crucial aspect was standardization, especially in a society spanning England, where messengers and agents often didn't know one another. This level of organization and resourcefulness surpassed the typical capabilities of a rebellion.

However, amidst the plethora of conspiracy theories and exaggerated ideas about secret societies, it's important to clarify that the Peasants' Revolt was not solely orchestrated by the Great Society. Various social and political factors fueled the uprising, the most prominent being the Black Death and its aftermath. The Plague's impact on the labor market significantly contributed to the rebellion. It would be misleading to entertain notions like the intentional introduction of an epidemic by an organization to foment revolt. Similarly, this shadowy group couldn't be held responsible for the corruption within the church, or the oppressive taxes and laws imposed by the king's government.

Instead, the orchestrators behind the Peasants' Revolt appear to have opportunistically seized upon existing grievances and conditions. They skillfully articulated and amplified the people's longstanding problems, channeling blame and anger toward their own objectives. The fact that Wat Tyler was killed before the Revolt could fully achieve its aims means that the true intentions of this enigmatic leader and his organization will likely remain unknown. What is clear is that the guiding force behind the rebellion seemed to vanish with him, as the organizers retreated back into obscurity.

In our pursuit of understanding the so-called Great Society, we face a daunting challenge due to the vast time gap of nearly seven centuries that separates us from the events. Uncovering concrete evidence is an arduous task. Only a fraction of the documents from that era have survived to the present day, and those that did are often biased, written from the perspective of the authorities. The secret society in question displayed remarkable skill in eluding government detection. Consequently, modern-day investigators are significantly disadvantaged. We are left with traces and imprints of the organization rather than definitive proof. We can infer their existence based on the historical context, the prevailing environment, and the government's responses, rather than relying on a single compelling piece of evidence. There is no indisputable proof, no smoking gun. The sources merely allude to 'a'

Great Society, refusing to use the definitive article 'the.' The label "Great Society" is employed out of convenience due to the absence of a better term.

Moreover, attempting to prove the existence of a secret society appears contradictory by nature. For a secret society to be truly successful, it would remain unknown to anyone outside its membership. Hence, there are no official records of any secret society in medieval England, except for the Lollards, whose work is only loosely related to this matter.

Addressing the connection to the Ancient Order of the Free and Accepted Masons, it's crucial to note that there is no contemporary documentation confirming the Freemasons' involvement in the rebellion. Likewise, there is no evidence to disprove this claim, although the burden of proof lies with those asserting such a connection. Instead, the links between the Freemasons and the uprising emerge from events a few years later, adding another layer of complexity to this historical puzzle.

Following the year 1717, there was a significant change in how the Masons operated. As we will explain later, they emerged from secrecy and became a public organization. It was during this period that the Freemasons became a verified group. Despite this, writers have attempted to trace the Freemasons' origins even further back in time. A quick online search or a glance through less rigorously researched books on the topic will mention figures like Pythagoras and Julius Caesar as members of the order, or possibly Grandmasters. However, these claims lack substantial evidence and are essentially imaginative speculations. Such ideas are not worth discussing in detail, aside from acknowledging their speculative nature.

Some more cautious suggestions propose figures such as King Solomon, the builder of Temple Mount, and suggest that his temple was the first Masonic structure. Modern historians dismiss this notion as mere fantasy. Nevertheless, it is possible to trace the Freemasons' lineage back many centuries before they became publicly known.

Many historians believe the origins of the organization now known as the Freemasons can be found in medieval times. During this era, it is believed that stone masons and other professionals formed guilds (a historically verified fact) and that these guilds later evolved into secretive societies. This version of the Freemasons' origin is widely accepted. The clear etymological connection between a masons' guild and the Freemasons supports this idea. So, how does this relate to the Peasants' Revolt and the Great Society that might have orchestrated it all?

Historians first point to the alleged leader of the rebels, Walter the Tyler (to use his full name). In England at that time, surnames often indicated a person's profession, especially when professions were passed down from one generation to another within a family. In small communities where professions persisted for generations, such names held significance. Although the modern meaning of surnames has changed, examining Wat Tyler's surname suggests that he was likely a tradesman or came from a family of skilled tradespeople, possibly tylers (tilers).

Wat Tyler stands out as a captivating figure in English history, seemingly appearing out of nowhere to lead one of the largest rebellions in the country's history. He rallied 100,000 peasants in a march against the aristocracy, causing widespread destruction, burning records, and executing prominent figures, including the Archbishop of Canterbury and the prior of the Knights Hospitallers. However, his moment in the spotlight was short-lived; within eight days of rising to prominence, he was captured, executed, and his head displayed on London Bridge. Prior to his sudden rise, little was known about him, but after his death, he became a legendary figure.

Some theories suggest that Wat Tyler might have used a false name. Despite his name implying a background in roof tiling, his evident military expertise and leadership skills make this origin story seem irrelevant. Instead, it is possible that he intentionally chose the name 'Tyler' to convey his position and significance to those aware of its relevance.

Here, it is necessary to delve into Masonic law. For the uninitiated, a Masonic Lodge follows a well-defined organizational structure, with specific titles corresponding to distinct roles and responsibilities. 'Tyler' is one such title. Within a Masonic Lodge, the Tyler serves as the sentry and enforcer, akin to a sergeant-at-arms. Their duties include screening potential members, verifying credentials, ensuring the security of the meeting place, and standing guard outside the room with a drawn sword during meetings. In contemporary terms, it is largely a ceremonial role, but in the secretive societies of the past, operating outside the law, it held vital importance. To Masons, the name 'Tyler' carries a specific meaning.

Considering the potential connection between the Great Society and the group that would eventually become the Freemasons, the significance of Wat the Tyler's name becomes more apparent. To those privy to the Masonic symbolism, Wat Tyler's emergence as the leader of the rebellion could have been a secret signal—an indication that he was an ordained military leader, the one destined to wield the sword and enforce discipline, ensuring military success. While this connection remains tenuous and speculative, it adds an intriguing layer to the historical narrative.

At a comparable level, there is a notion that Yorkshire played a significant role in the uprising, particularly in the city of York. York has historically been a crucial center for Masonry, with Masons as recently as the 18th century firmly believing that the York Lodge is the oldest in the country. According to their accounts, the Lodge's establishment dates back to the construction of York Cathedral in medieval times. Throughout the 18th century, the York Lodge played a pivotal role in Freemasonry. Displeased by the decision of London Lodges to publicly acknowledge their existence in 1717, the York Lodge spent the next decade distancing itself from their counterparts in the south and asserting their right to operate independently. They claimed this significance and privilege had been inherent to the York Lodge since ancient times.

Moreover, York's unique status in Freemasonry is exemplified by the modern belief, especially among American Masons, that the York branch of Masonry is the most authentic and aligned with Masonic traditions.

Undoubtedly, the rebellion shared ideological similarities with many Masonic principles. Viewing the Revolt from a broader perspective, the rejection of serfdom and the determination to attain freedom and break free from oppressive power structures resonate strongly with Masonic ideals. One of the central tenets of the Masonic order, known as the Landmarks of Freemasonry, stipulates that a Mason must be a "free man born of a free mother." Serfdom, it appears, would contradict this principle. The fact that, by the end of the 15th century, nearly every man in England could be considered "free" has been cited by some as evidence suggesting the antiquity of Masonry as a concept. However, the Peasants' Revolt being a demonstration in favor of Masonic ideals is not definitive proof that any Great Society could be considered a precursor or an early version of the Freemasons. Nonetheless, it does contribute depth to the argument that the Masons might have existed and held influence long before the commonly accepted timeline.

Possibly the most compelling evidence tying these various threads together can be found by examining a different society altogether. Understanding the potential earliest glimpses of a Masonic secret society might be elucidated through the existence of the Knights Hospitallers. The rebels' numerous attacks on Hospitaller properties and the execution of their leader, Sir Robert Hales, are highly significant. Consider the case of George de Donesby. Despite hailing from Lincolnshire, he was apprehended some 200 miles from his home and confessed to being a member of the so-called Great Society. What makes this noteworthy is that the aggrieved peasants in his hometown were particularly upset about the conduct of their local lords and had ceased paying taxes, which would have eventually ended up in a manor controlled by the Hospitallers. He stands out as one of the few individuals directly linked to the existence of the Great Society and harbored clear resentment against the Knights Hospitallers' structure and authority.

Certainly, the series of attacks carried out by the rioters on Hospitaller properties clearly reveals a deliberate and agenda-driven motive. For instance, when the rioters ventured north of London into Highbury, they specifically targeted the newly rebuilt manor of the Hospitallers, indicating them as natural enemies of the revolt. Amidst numerous potential targets in the heart of London, the rebels went out of their way, traveling six miles, to attack Hospitaller property. Similar incidents occurred nationwide, where rioters made special efforts to target these properties. In Cambridge, for instance, men rode ten miles off their route to burn down another Hospitaller manor.

It has long been argued that the Peasants' Revolt was, in part, a protest against the corruption within the church. If this is indeed true, the rebels certainly directed their attacks at churches and religious buildings, especially when burning records that could be used by the government to perpetuate serfdom. Notably, the churches attacked were disproportionately owned and operated by the Hospitallers. The rebels purposefully sought out and burned down only the properties belonging to these Knights, while other attacks were sporadic crimes of opportunity. Rarely did the rebels deviate from their intended path except to attack Hospitaller properties.

Curiously, the one church the rebels seemed reluctant to burn down was the Hospitaller church near Fleet Street. Instead, they removed all available records from the building and burned them in the street. Was it mere chance that this particular property had once been favored by the Knights Templar? Could there have been a desire to preserve this church above all others, despite the presence of the Hospitallers? The church had been consecrated in 1185 by Heraclius, the then-patriarch of the holy city of Jerusalem, in the name of the Knights Templar. Interestingly, the same patriarch had also consecrated the Hospitallers' property in Clerkenwell. However, as that property had not previously belonged to the Templars, the rebels had no qualms about burning it down. Was it a coincidence that the rebels' attacks were so distinctly focused on one of the oldest foes of the Knights Templar? Could this have been an act of retaliation from a group that had seemingly been forced into hiding and pushed out of existence?

Even subtle details, such as the choice of uniform among many rebels, hint at a possible Templar influence. In towns like Scarborough, Beverly, and York, the rebels wore a white shawl with a hood and a red decorative touch. This choice not only indicates premeditation — it would have been difficult to produce 500 of these on the spot and distribute them over long distances — but also closely resembles the clothing worn by the Templars themselves: a white mantle with a red cross.

A significant connection emerges from the death of Jack Strawe, one of the rebel army's highest-ranking members and a close associate of Wat Tyler. Captured and brought to London, Strawe faced a death sentence for his role in organizing the rebellion. Authorities attempted to extract a confession from him and offered him a Christian burial and three years' worth of masses in exchange for revealing the rebellion's "true purpose." Strawe agreed and confessed that the plan was not just to gather a massive crowd of common people and execute opposing lords but also to obliterate the Hospitallers — not just their property, but their entire organization. While the reason for this intense animosity was unspecified, there appears to be a clear answer to the question of who could have harbored such hatred toward the Hospitallers.

This deep-seated hostility had been brewing for decades. Since the official disbandment of the Knights Templar in 1312, after years of torture and investigation, questions arose about what should be done with the Templars' vast business holdings. Many who sought to dismantle the Templars desired their wealth, and they took it. One of the primary beneficiaries, however, was the Knights Hospitaller. It is understandable why a group forced into secrecy might resent and despise one of their chief rivals. Could this resentment have driven the destruction of Hospitaller property and the execution of the grand prior of the order, Robert Hales? Did the Templars harbor a similar grudge against the Catholic Church, the organization that had founded and then abandoned them? Could this resentment have led them to disregard sacred sacraments, ancient sanctuary rites, and even execute the Archbishop of Canterbury? It is evident that the Templars might have held animosity towards both institutions, and the Peasants' Revolt provided them with an opportunity for revenge.

In fact, there appears to be a direct reference to the Templars in the chronicles from Bury St. Edmunds, one of the bloodiest sites of the Revolt that was notably excluded from the amnesty. Records from the time, highlighted in Antonia Gransden's book, suggest a particular resentment against the Templars. The chronicles reimagined some of the Templars' heroic tales, portraying them as traitorous individuals instead of tragic heroes. These accounts even accused the Templars of poisoning the King of Cyprus and his family. Such accusations could have enraged a hidden Templar faction and hinted at the propaganda campaign initiated following the Templars' downfall. Bury St. Edmunds, the source of some of the most extreme falsehoods about the Templars, might have borne the brunt of violence due to the actions of the Benedictine monks.

All these speculations lead us to a crucial question: although the Peasants' Revolt is commonly seen as a failure, is this assessment accurate? If there was indeed a Great Society, possibly descended from the Knights Templar, providing guidance, expertise, and motivation, could the Revolt have been a success for those working behind the scenes?

If we consider the perspective of the so-called Great Society, assuming a connection to the Templars, was the destruction of Hospitaller, Crown, and Church properties one of the primary goals of the rebellion? If so, then there might have been a considerable degree of success. The extensive destruction of valuable properties, the annihilation of records, and the removal of wealth from notable enemies of the Templars could suggest that, from the Templar standpoint, the Revolt achieved significant objectives.

However, this scenario is hard to believe. Entertaining the notion that the Templars were the Great Society, or at least its foundational layer, raises questions about how an order that had been destroyed or forced underground for nearly seventy years could wield such influence. Many of their key leaders were executed during the Templar purge, and those knights who remained would have aged considerably. For instance, individuals who were twenty years old at the time of the Templar suppression would have been nearing ninety by the time of the Revolt. At best, they would have been lower-ranking members. It seems improbable that these individuals, especially without resorting to wild theories like the Templars owning the Holy Grail and its supposed life-extending properties, could live long enough to inspire a rebellion.

Similarly, the idea that the Templars could perpetuate their influence in secret over multiple generations, maintaining an enduring thirst for revenge, appears equally unlikely. Could such a clandestine society remain hidden in England for nearly seventy years, positioning itself strategically to exploit societal changes and circumstances that eventually led to the Peasants' Revolt?

Stepping away from the complexities of the narrative for a moment, let's examine the factual aspects:

There appears to have been a loosely organized group of individuals sympathetic to the Templars in England around the time of their dissolution. This is evident in the higher number of members who managed to evade capture in England compared to other countries. When the crown and the church collaborated to locate surviving Templars, they only found three members.

Among the Templars captured during the initial wave of arrests in England, many successfully escaped from prison. This indicates that they received assistance, either from insiders or outsiders.

The initial arrests in England occurred three months after the order to dissolve the Templars was issued on the continent. This window allowed the Templars in England to make preparations and establish their legacy and hiding places.

During this three-month period, it is plausible that the Templars in England established a new organization, a loosely structured group aimed at assisting them in response to the Pope's decree.

If such an organization did exist, it would have been founded with the substantial resources the Templars had at their disposal, necessary to sustain their cause long after the original members had passed. Consequently, it would have had ample funding and likely evolved over successive generations.

For such an organization to endure over an extended period, employing straightforward goals and objectives would enable them to maintain focus, even in the face of loose organization and the risk of discovery.

However, the question remains: where could such an organization thrive? Is it conceivable to establish a connection between the downfall of the Templars, the uprising of the Great Society, and the subsequent emergence of the Freemasons? We've begun to explore how these three entities might plausibly share common motives, and as we'll eventually uncover, they also seem to share much of the same ideology. Remarkably, in the future, the Freemasons would even incorporate numerous words and phrases from the Templars into their own practices. To unravel this mystery, our focus must shift north of the border. It appears that the key to understanding all three organizations lies in Scotland.

7

Chapter 6: Scottish Origins

Scotland appears to be the crucial link connecting the Freemasons and the Knights Templar. It is in Scotland that we find both the downfall of the Templars and the emergence of the Masons, although the precise nature of this transition remains unclear and challenging to discern. Depending on the source, this shift could have occurred over years, decades, or even centuries. In the upcoming chapter, we will delve into understanding how the Templars might have laid the groundwork for the organization that would eventually become the Freemasons. We will also explore the relationship between this development, the Great Society, and the Peasants' Revolt. To unravel this mystery, it's essential to examine the political climate in Scotland.

Historically, the relationship between Scotland and England has been marked by deep animosity. Much of this tension can be attributed to Edward I, known as the Hammer of the Scots, who dedicated a significant portion of his life to dealing with issues in the north. While we won't delve deeply into the intricacies of Edward's wars with Scotland, a brief overview is necessary to provide context.

In essence, Scotland desired independence from English rule, a prospect vehemently opposed by England. Although there was a sort of understanding between the Lords of Scotland and the English crown, the Scottish people were dissatisfied. From their midst emerged a figure: William Wallace. Wallace, immortalized in modern films, is widely recognized for his fight for freedom. He became one of Scotland's most accomplished military leaders, successfully leading Scottish armies against significantly larger English forces. By the end of 1297, Wallace had achieved notable victories, making a significant impact on the struggle against English domination.

Edward I and Wallace engaged in fierce battles over the years, set against a backdrop of a larger geopolitical struggle. Scotland sought alliances with France and the Vatican to secure its independence, while England, under Edward I, also pursued diplomatic engagements, sealing a pact with France in 1303. Edward I, known for his strategic use of the Templar Knights, eventually gained the upper hand by convincing fellow Scots to betray Wallace. Wallace was captured, brutally executed, and Edward I earned the moniker that would adorn his tombstone - the Hammer of the Scots.

In the wake of Edward I's death, subsequent monarchs faced a precarious situation. Edward II inherited a hostile Scotland led by Robert the Bruce, a fierce advocate for Scottish independence. To the south, Edward II lacked the prowess of his predecessor, weakening England's position. Additionally, Edward I's favorable stance towards the Templars had shielded them from Philip of France's aggression. However, with Edward I gone, the Templars lost their protection. Philip, seizing the opportunity, collaborated with the Vatican to launch a campaign against the Templars.

This scenario led to two entities, Scotland and the Knights Templar, sharing common grievances. Both had felt betrayed by France and the Vatican. With Edward I gone, the Templars lost their privileged status in England and were pursued relentlessly by Philip's forces and the church. Forced into hiding, the Templars, with their wealth and knowledge, might have found refuge in Scotland, a land sharing similar enemies, effectively making them potential allies.

After the Vatican issued orders for the outlawing of the Knights Templar, different European countries responded in diverse ways. In Paris, Templars faced brutal treatment; leaders, including the grand master, were tempted to go to France before the order was issued, resulting in their execution, and many Templars were burned alive on a single day. However, in Spain and Portugal, where Muslim invaders threatened the Iberian Peninsula, local branches of the church conducted their own inquisition into the Templars. These Templars were found innocent and were rebranded as the Knights of Christ, reporting to the local king instead of the pope.

In Germany, the Templar leader Hugo of Gumbach defiantly proclaimed the innocence of the Templars, challenging accusations and offering trial by combat, which quickly ended the accusations against them. On Cyprus, the Templars, based at their headquarters, resisted the papal instructions. The Prince of Cyprus, despite papal pressure, acknowledged the Templars' innocence in trials, frustrating the pope's intentions.

Even in France, Philip's plans to seize the Templars' wealth faced challenges. The expected riches were missing, and the Templar fleet, one of Europe's largest, had vanished from La Rochelle. The remaining wealth was transferred to the Hospitallers, except in the Iberian Peninsula due to the ongoing threat from Muslim forces. Pope Clement V decided to please various parties: he permitted local monarchs to recover expenses spent on Templar arrests, torture, and prosecution, a move seen as an attempt to reconcile different interests and form the basis for future Crusades.

The treatment of the Templars varied across Europe, but the situation in Great Britain is particularly significant for our story. In England, the transition from a strong king to a weak one played a pivotal role in the events that unfolded.

King Edward II of England was notorious for his personal life. One well-known story revolves around his relationship with a young man named Piers Gaveston, a romance that strained Edward I's relationship with his son.

Despite Gaveston's banishment during Edward I's reign, Edward II recalled him upon becoming king, causing tension within the court. Gaveston's mocking of the king's advisors further fueled the aristocracy's discontent.

Amidst this domestic turmoil, papal orders concerning the Templars reached England. Pope Clement V and Philip of France urged the English to expedite the prosecution of the Templars. However, Edward II, influenced by his father's support for the Templars, initially doubted the charges against them. He sought support from other European monarchs, believing the accusations to be false. Before he could receive replies, the official papal decree arrived, leaving Edward with no choice but to comply.

Despite receiving the papal decree, King Edward II of England did not act immediately against the English Templars. Several months passed, giving the Templars ample time to make plans. When the king's men finally set out to apprehend the Templars, they discovered that the knights had vanished, along with their records and treasure. Upon Edward's departure to France for his marriage to twelve-year-old Princess Isabella, Piers Gaveston, Edward's lover, was left in charge. This arrangement alarmed the nobles, as Gaveston was overseeing the Templar prosecution but showed little enthusiasm for the task. The efforts to capture Templars were lackluster, with some of those caught managing to escape. The Templars in England, once captured, were not subjected to the same tortures as their counterparts on the continent, which angered the pope. In response, he dispatched his own torturers to England and threatened excommunication for anyone aiding the Templars. This action drove the remaining Templars further underground.

Scotland presented a different scenario. The pope's attempts to have Templars arrested in Scotland failed. Robert the Bruce, engaged in ongoing military struggles, preferred recruiting trained and useful military men, like armored knights, rather than punishing them. He showed disinterest in a potential Crusade, monastic military organizations, Philip of France, or the pope's orders. Robert allegedly disregarded the papal decree related to the Templars, which was never announced in Scotland, making it a legal sanctuary for fleeing Templars.

This meant that if any Templar knight found himself in a legal bind in England or Europe, he could expect sanctuary in Scotland, especially if he was willing to join Robert the Bruce's military. Trained knights were crucial for Scotland, whose cavalry was reportedly lacking in both numbers and quality at the time.

By 1313, England was facing a delicate situation. Tensions between Piers Gaveston and the nobles had resulted in Gaveston's execution. As the nobles sought to regain influence over Edward II, Philip of France, the king's father-in-law, advised Edward to affirm his allegiance to the church. This involved participating in the newly declared Vatican Crusade, an initiative aimed at reclaiming the Holy Land for Christendom. However, England's participation in the Crusade was impractical. Sending away the country's best fighters while Robert the Bruce continued his conquest in Scotland would jeopardize the progress made under Edward I's rule. While the Crusade was underway, Robert was steadily recapturing castles in Scotland. To regain control and assert his authority, Edward had to face the Scottish challenge directly.

Edward assembled an army of 25,000 men to march north and subdue Scotland once and for all. His forces included 5,000 cavalry and 10,000 archers. In response, Robert the Bruce managed to gather 10,000 troops. Aware of the approaching English forces, Robert strategically chose the battlefield long before Edward and his army arrived. While the English soldiers marched exhaustingly, growing tired and hungry, the Scottish soldiers fortified their position, ensuring they were well-fed and refreshed. Robert positioned his army between the advancing English troops from the south and one of the few remaining English strongholds in the region, Stirling Castle. This strategic move prevented Edward from resupplying his forces before facing the Scottish army.

In strategizing the battle, Robert the Bruce applied lessons from William

Wallace. He created potholes on the field to impede the English knights and stationed men armed with twelve-foot spears, concealed under cover and camouflaged. Wallace had met betrayal from his own cavalry, so Robert, wanting to avoid a similar fate, positioned himself at the forefront of Scotland's armored knights. Legend has it that these cavalrymen included fugitive Templars who had fled north, swearing allegiance to Robert. The battle offered them a chance for revenge against the man who had betrayed them to the pope.

The battle became a historic Scottish victory. Outflanked, the English army panicked and fled. A pivotal moment occurred when non-combatants from the Scottish camp—women, boys, and others—picked up arms and overwhelmed the English, mistaken for fresh Scottish reinforcements. The fleeing English forces were completely routed, with England losing up to 15,000 men, while Scottish casualties were only around 4,000. This resounding victory marked the end of English rule over Scotland for nearly 400 years.

Moreover, the magnitude of the English defeat plunged Edward II's kingdom into chaos. Ambitious nobles, disenchanted with their inept ruler, seized more power for themselves. Law and order collapsed, leading to the rise of outlaw heroes like Robin Hood, who resisted corrupt rulers and preyed on the wealthy. The consequences of this defeat were so severe for Edward II that he lost his throne. Betrayed by his wife and nobles, he was executed in a brutal manner—having a red-hot iron spit thrust into his rectum. Edward III, a teenager at the time, succeeded him, and his reign would pave the way for the eventual Peasants' Revolt.

The disastrous reign of Edward II had significant implications for the Templars and their future in Scotland. With the loss of Scotland for centuries and the persecution they faced in England, the outlawed Templars found refuge in Scotland. Their arrival in this new land necessitated secrecy, given their existence was considered heretical. However, their wealth, military knowledge, and presence became valuable assets for the Scottish king.

In this clandestine existence, the Templars had to adapt and repurpose their organization. They transitioned from being a military order of knights to becoming a covert secret society. Their agenda shifted, focusing on vengeance and clandestine operations. As fugitives, they transformed into individuals in hiding, adopting a cold and calculated approach to achieve their goals. Behind the scenes, they evolved into a powerful secret society, maintaining their ambitions and possibly laying the groundwork for what would later be known as the Great Society, which would trouble England seven decades later.

8

Chapter 7: Fugitives

On the surface, the escape plan of the Knights Templar seemed well-organized and poised for success. Templars outside of Italy and France, such as those in England and Cyprus, were granted up to three months to strategize their getaway. Their considerable wealth, political connections, and access to various means of transportation, particularly their fleet, created a favorable environment for their escape. These factors have led many to believe that the Templars possessed the essential organizational resources to evade persecution effectively. While some high-ranking Templars faced execution, and many others endured torture and death, the overall attempt to obliterate the Templars appeared to have fallen short.

However, this didn't mean that the Templars had it easy. They had been officially condemned by the Church, resulting in a seemingly universal ban across Europe. The entire Christian world was seemingly opposed to their presence, as decreed by the Pope. Everywhere they went was hostile territory. Considering that a significant portion of European land was owned by various church-affiliated entities, none of whom were particularly sympathetic to the Templars, most regions became perilous for Templar members. Their distinct attire, hairstyles, mannerisms, and predominantly French-speaking nature made it challenging for them to blend in with the locals, further complicating their efforts to go into hiding.

Consequently, a fugitive Templar required assistance. If they were to adopt a new identity, which was undoubtedly essential, they needed someone to vouch for their new persona. In a time when towns and cities were much smaller than they are today (for instance, London had a population of 25,000 and was the largest city in England), this had to be accomplished on a personal level. The Templars needed allies.

This is where we observe a remarkable resemblance between the sudden needs of the Templars and one of the ancient rules of Freemasonry. Known as one of the Old Charges of the Masons, the rule states that no brother should enter a town unless he can do so in the company of another brother who can vouch for him or "witness" on his behalf. Because authorities had the authority to apprehend strangers without such endorsement, there exists a clear historical precedent for an old rule that is now predominantly symbolic. Indeed, during the five years between the initial announcement of the Pope's anti-Templar order and the official dissolution of the organization, as well as the slowed or delayed processes in certain countries, there was ample time for the Templars to establish a covert system of checks and balances. Code words and passphrases could signify trust, with their knowledge discreetly disseminated within the Templar community before they went into hiding. By the time the authorities eventually came searching for them, these checks and balances could assist the outlawed Templars in remaining concealed.

The fate of the Templar fleet has become a central element in the story we're exploring. Numerous theories have emerged regarding what happened to these ships after they left La Rochelle and what valuable cargo they might have been carrying. While some imaginative accounts include legendary items like the Holy Grail and religious relics, it's more plausible that the Templars' wealth and knowledge were their true treasures. With members from diverse backgrounds and countries, the Templars possessed extensive information about various people, stored within their ranks. Many speculate that this wealth of knowledge, combined with their traditional riches, would merge with another society, fusing the Templars' forbidden knowledge with the emerging principles of stone masons, particularly the Freemasons.

At first glance, the idea that the Knights Templar and the Freemasons share a common heritage might seem incredible and wishful. After all, these are two of history's most secretive groups. However, delving into the medieval European context, especially in England, reveals an ideal environment for the emergence of clandestine organizations. Shared grievances, similar patterns, and mysterious histories connect both groups. Moreover, there's more than mere speculation linking the two societies.

Traditionally, Freemasonry's history traces back to guild-like organizations that regulated and promoted the work of tradesmen. While this is well-documented, it's not incompatible with the idea that the Templars influenced early masonry guilds. Consider the Old Charge of Freemasonry, one of the organization's oldest pledges. This rule requires members not to disclose any secrets of fellow members that could endanger their lives or property. While this rule might seem irrelevant for an organization focused on tradesmen, it becomes crucial for a fugitive Templar. The secrets held by stonemasons could indeed be matters of life and death for those associated with the Templars. This historical context suggests a more intricate connection between the Templars and the Freemasons than mere speculation.

A compelling theory emerges, suggesting that the fugitive Knights Templar found a connection with the earliest Freemasons, leading to the incorporation of Templar rituals and ideas into the Freemasons' rules and practices. While this idea might seem outrageous at first, delving into historical records offers increasing support for this theory.

In the 14th century, the Templars faced formidable adversaries: the monarchy, the church, and the Knights Hospitallers. Among these, the church posed the most significant challenge to the fugitive Templars. Throughout their existence, the Knights Templar had been a religious organization, deeply rooted in Christianity and answerable only to the pope and God. However, they were betrayed by the very institution they served. The church declared them outlaws and heretics, severing their connection to their spiritual leader, as their grand master was executed on the orders of the pope.

Balancing their deep faith with this profound betrayal must have been incredibly challenging for the Templars. In secret, it is not surprising that they grew to resent the Catholic Church, despising the corruption and greed it had come to symbolize. These feelings, however, remained private. During that era, there was no alternative belief system. The Vatican held a monopoly on faith in Western Europe. While the seeds of the future Protestant Reformation had been planted, they had yet to flourish into a genuine Christian alternative. The fact that the Templars were compelled, or perhaps forced, to harbor such thoughts in absolute secrecy became fundamental to their resentment of the church and how it manifested in their actions.

Examining the beliefs of the Freemasons provides valuable insights into their approach to religion. Within the Freemasons, there is a fundamental principle that serves as the cornerstone of the entire society. This core tenet revolves around the acknowledgment of the existence of one Supreme Being. To become a member, a Freemason must affirm their faith in this higher power. However, the society does not regulate religious practices beyond this initial belief. How an individual chooses to practice their faith is not a matter of concern for the Freemasons. In fact, members are expressly prohibited from discussing their religious beliefs or attempting to convert others to their particular viewpoint while inside the Lodge. This foundational rule has stood the test of time, enduring longer than any other regulation and serving as the bedrock of Freemasonry.

This rule becomes intriguing when considered in light of potential Templar influence. During that era, the religious beliefs of a stonemason or trades-man were generally inconsequential, as people were expected to follow the Vatican's guidance due to the Church's dominant influence. Thus, such a rule might seem unnecessary for a typical secret society. However, for the Templars, who found themselves in a world marked by self-doubt and resentment, this rule made perfect sense. Although they would not have abandoned their belief in God as a monastic order, their recent experiences with the Vatican would likely have opened their minds to alternative forms of religious practice. Discussing such matters could have posed a significant danger for them. Therefore, it made sense for religious discussions to be off-limits within the society. By ensuring that all members believed in a Supreme Being and refraining from delving into religious topics, this rule offered a level of protection for potential Templars, a safeguard not merely applicable to stonemasons.

This connection between Freemasonry's ancient principles and the possible integration of fugitive Templars into the organization becomes apparent when scrutinizing the society's oldest rules and regulations. Many of these guidelines seem tailored to provide refuge for Templars seeking asylum from authorities and integrating them discreetly into the Freemasons. However, it is essential to emphasize repeatedly that despite these compelling links and theories, concrete historical evidence supporting such ties remains elusive. No definitive document or record has been found to suggest the existence of a secret society founded by Templars in hiding. Consequently, most of the connections we uncover and the theories we formulate remain speculative. Nevertheless, this ongoing inquiry continues to fuel curiosity and exploration.

Understanding the religious beliefs of the Freemasons remains a challenging task. Medieval guilds, including stone masons' guilds, were inherently religious organizations, deeply devoted to the church. These guilds, spread across Europe, upheld various religious practices, from honoring patron saints and staging religious performances to supporting local churches and commissioning religious artworks. They were closely integrated into their communities and operated in harmony with the church. Given this context, it raises a perplexing question: why did a specific guild, the Freemasons, adopt a uniquely secular and secretive approach to religious matters? What led them to establish a rule that presupposed Christianity yet allowed for members of other religions, excluding only atheists, a perspective almost alien to the medieval mindset?

The Masonic rule, requiring belief in a Supreme Being without delving into specific religious practices, raises even more questions as one delves deeper into the history of the Masons. The closer one examines, the more inquiries arise. However, the existence of this rule, especially when considering the potential influence of the Templars, seems to offer a near-perfect solution. It provides protection for the fugitive Templars who were fleeing the church's condemnation while still maintaining their religious identity as a monastic order. With newfound doubts about their faith, these Templars found refuge within the Freemasons' rule, serving as an ideal sanctuary. When fitting the pieces of this historical puzzle together, the connections appear seamless and logical, pointing towards a theory that, although nearly impossible to prove definitively, aligns all the facts cohesively.

Let's reconsider the fundamental aspects of this situation before drawing any conclusions:

The Knights Templar, originally devoted to the Catholic Church, were condemned by the Church itself.

They had ample time to prepare for hiding and possessed significant resources, skills, and knowledge aiding their escape.

The Templars had valid reasons to resent the church, monarchy, and the Knights Hospitaller following the papal decree.

Scotland, due to political circumstances, provided an ideal sanctuary for the Templars.

In the late 14th Century, a secretive group known as the Freemasons emerged, allegedly originating from medieval trade guilds. However, there is no documented evidence confirming the exact origins of this secret society.

The rules of the Freemasons appeared tailored for fugitive Templars seeking to avoid detection, many of which were irrelevant to the daily life of a late 14th Century stonemason.

Both the Freemasons and the Knights Templar held significance in their beliefs regarding the Temple of Solomon.

The Peasants' Revolt was orchestrated by a mysterious organization, the Great Society, which provided structural guidance and support to the rebellion.

The targets of the Peasants' Revolt were institutions, properties, and resources owned by groups considered enemies of the Knights Templar.

None of the members of the Great Society were apprehended or formally prosecuted.

When examining the evidence, it appears plausible to suggest that the Knights Templar, fleeing from authorities, could have influenced the foundational principles of what eventually became Freemasonry. These ideas surfaced during events like the Peasants' Revolt before fading away. Exploring all the similarities and parallels between the Freemasons and the fugitive Templars would require more space than available in this book. However, it leaves one with the sense that there might be more to this idea than what the limited historical evidence suggests. Secret societies, by their nature, remain shrouded in secrecy, making it nearly impossible to uncover the truth from a six-century distance. Nonetheless, speculation and investigation remain possible.

It's essential to keep this concept in mind as we delve into the early history of the Freemasons. Throughout the following sections of the book, considering how a Templar influence might have shaped the Freemasons' ideological path or guided them in a specific direction can be valuable. While definitive physical evidence is scarce, the preceding sections have laid the groundwork, suggesting that such a connection is not entirely implausible. As we progress toward the conclusion, the journey thus far should shed light on what lies ahead. While answering the question of the Knights Templar's fate might be elusive, we can explore whether the early years of the Freemasons were potentially influenced by such a group.

9

Chapter 8:The Emergence of Freemasonry

In contemporary times, Freemasonry operates on a global scale, not in a conspiratorial context where Masons are held responsible for geopolitical events, but as a vast international organization. In fact, the Freemasons constitute the largest fraternal organization worldwide. Their membership numbers nearly three million in the United States alone, with approximately 700,000 members in their birthplace, Britain, and an additional million members across the globe. The organization's magnitude has attracted significant attention, resulting in the production of an extensive body of literature—ranging from books and pamphlets to magazine articles and websites—totaling up to fifty thousand pieces. The book you are currently reading is just one of the numerous texts attempting to explore aspects of Freemasonry. Undoubtedly, Freemasonry is a global phenomenon.

Since the formal dissolution of the Knights Templar in 1312 and the occurrence of the Peasants' Revolt in 1381, the world has undergone substantial transformations. In 1717, Freemasonry chose to officially reveal itself to the public. Today, Freemasonry has evolved into an entirely different entity from its historical origins. Although the organization still retains vestiges of its original secretive nature, the widespread interest and available information have diminished its clandestine aura. This book, however, does not focus on contemporary Masonry; instead, it delves into the origins of the Freemasons and the potential influences on their early development.

Examining the history of the Masons poses challenges, particularly due to the writings by actual members. Historically, some authors attempted to include virtually any influential figure as a Masonic member and even placed early Masonic branches in ancient civilizations such as Egypt, Celtic Britain, and Persia. At one point, Masonic scholars engaged in a competition to make increasingly audacious claims. While such tendencies have subsided, they have left behind a confusing legacy for those seeking the truth.

Over time, historians have gradually scaled back their claims about the origins of the Freemasons. Initially, there were assertions connecting the first Masons to the founding of the Temple of Solomon, creating a supposed link between the Masons and the Templars. These claims were based on a few lines from the Master Mason's initiation ceremony. However, these lines, upon closer examination, do not align with the historical description of Solomon's Temple as presented in the Bible; instead, they appear to be more allegorical in nature.

While there is little concrete evidence linking the establishment of the Freemasons to Solomon's Temple, as acknowledged by modern Masonic historians, the possibility of Templar influence remains open. The connections drawn between the Temple of Solomon (which served as the verified headquarters of the Templars after the First Crusade) and the Freemasons appear to have originated from medieval guilds. The intriguing question arises: why would medieval tradesmen, individuals primarily concerned with tools, techniques, and materials, delve into allegorical interpretations of Christianity? Such queries only lead to further puzzlement.

In reality, only two organizations claim a significant association with the Temple of Solomon—the Freemasons and the Knights Templar. Is this a mere coincidence? Or could it be that the downfall of one organization contributed to the rise of the other, with both sharing essential beliefs, approaches, resources, tactics, adversaries, and ideologies?

The circumstances strongly suggest the latter scenario. The Templars in England had ample time to prepare themselves in 1307, coinciding with the fact that the newly crowned King Edward II was one of the weakest and most ineffective rulers in the country's history. Such vulnerable individuals would have been welcomed across the border in Scotland but would have had to remain concealed.

Certainly, the prolonged period of persecution endured by the Templars from 1307 to 1314, spanning seven years, served as a crucible that bound these fugitive knights together in secrecy. During their years in hiding, these individuals, brought together by shared adversity, could have grown akin to brothers. Their clandestine structure likely became more formalized and organized with each passing day. By the time the official persecution of the Templars came to an end, these hidden fugitives might have evolved into an entirely new secret society—one deeply rooted in the memory of past injustices. With their focus on resentment toward the church, the crown, and the Hospitallers, these fugitive Templars found themselves at the helm of a covert organization, even more clandestine than before, and one that could have established its base in Scotland.

The symbols and emblems of Freemasonry find straightforward explanations in the existence of the Templars. Take, for instance, the square and compass logo, which bears a striking resemblance to the seal of Solomon, representing the Templars' original home. By simplifying the Templar seal and removing its horizontal lines, one can discern a basic interpretation of the Masonic symbol. Additionally, the circles and mosaics commonly seen around Masonic Lodges are shared elements with Templar iconography. Everything—from the attire worn during Masonic rituals to the oaths sworn, the colors used, the signs employed, and nearly every aspect of Masonic ceremonies—can be traced back to the influence of the Knights Templar.

Historians have meticulously examined the rules and regulations of medieval tradesmen guilds throughout Europe. These documents, although typically mundane, differ significantly from the ordinances of the Freemasons. The rules of the Freemasons are not meant to be taken literally; rather, they appear to be figurative lessons, serving as a façade for what ostensibly seemed like a guild but had a concealed purpose: to safeguard the remaining members and ideologies of the Knights Templar.

In the 18th century, certain factions within the Masons even adopted the name 'Knights Templar' to signify an exclusive Christian group within the Freemasons. These undeniable connections exist, although it is challenging to discern how much is original and how much was later devised by the Masons, constructed deliberately in remembrance and respect for the Templars. The most compelling evidence often lies in the brief period between the downfall of the Templars and the emergence of secret Masonic Lodges.

As the Templars gradually disappeared and new members joined, the organization underwent transformations. The mutual protection provided by their codes and rules allowed past agendas and animosities to persist. Even before they formally adopted the name Freemasons—when they still operated as an extremely secretive society—they briefly entered the public consciousness by causing upheaval among their former adversaries during the Peasants' Revolt. This event stands as a pivotal moment in this narrative, showcasing the secret society that existed between the Templars and the Masons. During this period, the group was still evolving and maturing. The fact that it was only known as the Great Society highlights this transformation, emphasizing how little was known about the group at the time.

However intriguing these connections may seem, it's crucial to approach them with a demand for concrete evidence. While the facts might align with the theory, the lack of physical proof is a significant hurdle. The period from the early 14th century to the beginning of the 18th century marks a gap where official documentation of the Templars fades, and the emergence of the Freemasons begins. Exploring this gap is essential for understanding the theory's implications.

One pivotal moment during this period is the Peasants' Revolt of 1381. It's notable because it appears to bring these secretive activities to the surface. Various aspects of the rebellion, such as the targeting of the Hospitallers, the actions against the Archbishop of Canterbury, the breach into the Tower of London, the safeguarding of the Templar church, and the occasional mention of the Great Society, all offer links to either or both of these organizations. Walter the Tyler, with a name seemingly influenced by Masonic roots, exhibited military leadership akin to the Templars, indicating a potential connection. As the leader of a covert society endowed with substantial resources and influence, Tyler could have been one of the earliest Masons descending from the last Templars.

Even in the aftermath of the Peasants' Revolt, the presence of the Lollards in England adds to the intrigue. The Lollards, a religiously motivated secret society, operated beyond official records and conventional government structures. Although their connection to the Freemasons or Templars remains unclear, their existence demonstrates the possibility of a secret society thriving in medieval England. The Lollards persisted through the medieval age and into the Reformation era, occasionally resurfacing, such as during Sir John Oldcastle's 1414 revolt against the crown. These instances highlight the clandestine nature of such organizations, suggesting that secret societies could operate beneath the surface of medieval society, leaving subtle traces of their presence.

The existence of the Lollards stands as compelling evidence that secret societies could thrive in medieval England, wielding significant influence. Detailed accounts, such as Henry Kingston's report on Lollard activities in Leicester, provide a glimpse into a secret society that shared intriguing similarities with the Freemasons. The Lollards, who took St. John as their patron saint (akin to the Freemasons), held clandestine meetings, advocated ideas akin to Masonic principles (such as opposing lawsuits in debt cases), enjoyed protection from local knights, and faced persecution for heresy. This description not only serves as a potential precursor to Freemasonry but could even be seen as an early example of a similar covert organization in action, resembling a 14th-century Masonic Lodge.

This circumstantial evidence carries us forward to the 17th century. By this time, the Lollards appeared to have disbanded, yet reports of secret societies persisted. Historian C. V. Wedgwood, in a book about the reign of Charles I, documented Archbishop of Canterbury's reports about secret meetings taking place across the kingdom. These reports culminated in the arrest of a man named Trendall, who was preaching against the church's hierarchy in London. The Archbishop intended to burn Trendall at the stake, a method of punishing heretics that was nearly obsolete by that time. Although the Archbishop sought advice on conducting the burning, it appears the execution never occurred. Trendall, whose profession was listed as a stone mason, seemingly escaped the punishment. The incident leaves lingering questions, suggesting the possibility of influential networks or connections safeguarding Trendall, adding an air of mystery to the tale.

The emergence of Masonic principles can be traced through the works of prominent figures like John Locke and Francis Bacon. Both Locke and Bacon incorporated ideas in their writings that directly relate to Freemasonry. Locke, for instance, included specific measures in the constitution of South Carolina, such as restrictions on filing lawsuits for money, reflecting Masonic ideals. Bacon's concepts about religion and science, notably explored in his work "The New Atlantis," mirrored Masonic perspectives, envisioning a society built clandestinely on Masonic principles. References to Masonic ideas in literature during the 15th, 16th, and 17th centuries further indicate the growing influence of Freemasonry in England.

The notion of Templar influence on Freemasons is not new. In the early days of Freemasonry becoming public, there were accusations of Templar influence. The Rite of Strict Observance, a German Masonic branch in the 18th century, restructured Lodge organization and disclaimed Templar origins. According to this group, Templar fugitives had sought refuge in Scotland and aligned with a stone mason guild. Despite its brief existence, this branch rejected the supposed Templar connection. This perspective predates the ideas explored in this book.

Various theories propose links between Freemasons and the Knights Templar, often dismissed as either a Jesuit conspiracy to discredit the Masons or as fictional plot devices. These ideas typically hinge on accepting the false charges brought against the Templars by Prince Philip of France and the Vatican. Such claims attempt to associate the Freemasons with guilt by association, relying on a distorted version of history.

The debate about the connection between the Templars and the Freemasons persists, with staunch believers and skeptics arguing vehemently. Unfortunately, the intense arguments have hindered genuine investigations into the matter. The adamant denial of any link by skeptics has diminished the chances of uncovering the complete truth. Additionally, sensational and baseless claims, such as the Freemasons' supposed association with Celtic Druids, further confuse the issue, making it difficult to discern verifiable facts.

In the modern era, Freemasonry is no longer a secret society. There are numerous books providing detailed insights into their rituals. However, the mystery lies in their historical origins. Today, Freemasonry is often viewed as a social pastime, even though some ranks explicitly reference the Knights Templar. The Templar story is recounted to members, but it seems to be a routine retelling rather than something meant to inspire or educate. The true significance of the Templars to the Freemasons has been overshadowed by ritualistic practices, becoming just another part of their intricate history. Unfortunately, the real truth remains elusive.

10

Conclusion

In the early days of Christianity, believers had to conceal their faith due to religious persecution, exemplifying a secret society. They used symbols, like the fish, as a covert means of identification. The fish, once a survival tactic, became a Christian symbol, much like the Templars' and Freemasons' secrecy. This book presents substantial circumstantial evidence, suggesting the Knights Templar's downfall coincided with the formation of a secret society in Great Britain. Fugitive Templars possibly aligned with a Scottish masonic guild, adopting their symbols for disguise. Similar to guilds safeguarding trade secrets, Freemasonry sheltered Templars from authorities. Their ideas laid the foundation for Freemasonry, echoing the enduring legacy of Templar influences, akin to the fish symbol in churches worldwide. While modern Freemasonry is no longer secretive like early Christianity, understanding their historical origins is essential. This exploration avoids conspiracies, focusing on historical hints, inviting curiosity about the Templar-Freemason connection. Instead of viewing Freemasons as a modern threat, understanding their centuries-old evolution enriches our perspective, even if the complete truth remains elusive. Uncovering a secret society's history, even with these hints, exceeds typical expectations.

www.ingramcontent.com/pod-product-compliance
Lightning Source LLC
LaVergne TN
LVHW010659200726
843507LV00011B/1946